Who Do You Say That I Am?

Shocking Statements About Jesus From Prominent Jews

By

Steve Schwartz

Who Do You Say That I Am?

Published by
Innovo Publishing, LLC.

Copyright © 2009 by Steve Schwartz
All rights reserved.

No part of this publication may be reproduced, stored in a retrieval system or transmitted in any form or by any means electronic, mechanical, photocopying, recording or otherwise, without the prior written permission of the author.

ISBN 13: 978-0-9815403-8-2
ISBN 10: 0-9815403-8-4

Cover Design & Interior Layout: Innovo Publishing, LLC

Printed in the United States of America
U.S. Printing History

First Edition: March 2009

Shalom!

I dedicate this book to my family – a family divided by our very different answers to Jesus' question: *Who do you say that I am?* I also dedicate this book to my Jewish readers. I pray that you will keep an open mind and that you will weigh the evidence carefully as you seek to answer Jesus' question for yourself. Lastly, I dedicate this book to my Christian friends who love the Jewish people and the Jewish Messiah. Thanks to people like you, I learned about the Messiah who laid down his life so that I might enjoy eternal life in God's presence.

Foreword

I am what you would call a skeptic. When I tell people I'm from Missouri – the "Show Me" state – I really mean it. I was born and raised in a suburb of St. Louis, and I spent the first 20 years of my life in Missouri.

There's no doubt about it – I'm a doubting Thomas. Whenever I receive an e-mail containing what I believe may be an urban legend, I always check out the facts before forwarding the e-mail to anyone else. After all, I don't want to pass along anything that I haven't verified to be true.

Why am I telling you all this? Because I was very skeptical when a Christian friend told me that Jesus was – and is – the Jewish Messiah.

It took me over a year of intensive study before I came to believe that the answer to the title of this book is: *Jesus is the Messiah, the Son of the Living God.* I literally read hundreds of books and booklets, most of which were critical of Jesus' claim to be the Messiah.

But as a journalist and writer, I knew how to do research, and I decided to follow the evidence – even if it took me in a direction I didn't want to go. Though I'm a skeptic, at least I'm an honest skeptic. So when the overwhelming evidence took me to the feet of Jesus, I gave up the fight and surrendered.

Over the ensuing 35 years, some of my Jewish friends have told me I've been brainwashed. Now, I have to ask how they could charge me with something like that. After all, I had the intellectual integrity to examine *both* sides of the issue. Had they done that?

I feel that if anyone has been brainwashed, it's those who are exposed to only one side of the story. They believe what they believe because that's what they've been taught. Sadly, too many people nowadays don't want to make the effort or take the time to examine both sides of an issue like this.

That's exactly why I wrote this book! I don't expect anyone to study three hours a day for over a year to see whether Jesus is the

Messiah or an imposter. But I feel that anyone can spend an hour or two reading this book.

Perhaps you'll come to the same conclusion that I did. Perhaps not. But at least you'll be able to say you've looked at both sides.

- Steve Schwartz, March 2009

TABLE OF CONTENTS

INTRODUCTION 1

   How Jewish Scholars Answer the Question 7

   How Jewish Authors Answer the Question 15

   How Will You Answer the Question? 21

FOOTNOTES 29

BONUS RELEASE: Dear Rabbi, Tell Me About Jesus 33

INTRODUCTION 35

   Letter #1: My First Letter to the Rabbi 37

   Letter #2: The Rabbi's Response 41

   Letter #3: My Response to the Rabbi 45

   Letter #4: The Rabbi's Final Response to Me 57

   Letter #5: My Final Response to the Rabbi 59

Postscript 64

The Old Testament Chapter Banned from the Synagogue 65

Isaiah 53 67

NOTES 69

About the Author 72

INTRODUCTION

"Who do you say that I am?"

Nearly 2,000 years ago, a man from Nazareth posed this question to his Jewish followers and received the immediate reply, "You are the Messiah, the Son of the living God."

Today, Jesus of Nazareth still has many Jewish followers, joined by multitudes of gentiles who believe that he was and is the Messiah of both Israel and the world.

Most Jewish people today, however, don't know how they would answer that question, because they've never taken a close look at Jesus. They have been taught to believe that Jesus has no relevance for them. At best, they believe that Jesus is the Messiah of the gentiles but that there is no need for Jewish people to answer the question Jesus asked so long ago.

It is important to note, however, that many Jewish authorities – rabbis, authors, historians, statesmen and theologians – were not ashamed to take a long, hard look at the man from Nazareth. And even though most of them did not accept Jesus as their long-awaited Messiah, they expressed their highest regards for him. And they made it clear that Jesus is of great importance to Jewish people.

Historians are agreed that the life of this one man did more to change the course of world history than any other person who ever lived. How ironic and sad that the great majority of Jewish people – who are second to none in knowledge and learning – are, for the most part, ignorant of this first-century Jewish man.

This book will help you get a better picture of Jesus *from the Jewish perspective*. It presents the surprising views of Jewish personalities of the past and present. To give you an idea of what you'll be encountering in these pages, here is a sampling of how some well-respected Jewish philosophers, authors and rabbis have answered Jesus' question: "Who do you say that I am?"

Joseph Klausner, author: "Jesus was a Jew and a Jew he remained till his last breath. His one idea was to implant within his nation the idea of the coming of the Messiah and, by repentance and good works, hasten the 'end' ... In all this, Jesus is the most Jewish of Jews, more Jewish than Simeon ben Shetah, more Jewish even than Hillel."[1]

Heinrich Graetz, considered by many to be the greatest of Jewish historians: "Like Hillel, Jesus looked on the promotion of peace and forgiveness of injuries as the highest forms of virtue. His whole being was permeated by that deeper religion which contributed to the mildness of his face. He has made humanity honour; he has carried the highest wisdom to the homes of the lowly and the ignorant of the world. He has carried it beyond all barriers of schools and temples, and for this, only, he had to die a death of shame. The redeemer of the poor, the teacher of the ignorant, the friend of all that faint with toil and are oppressed with cares must die on the cross. Over the supreme tragedy let the angel of sorrow spread his wings. Veil thy face, sun! Be darkened, sky! Let the earth tremble and men mourn in tears! The most angelic of men, the most loving of teachers, the meek and humble prophet is to die by the death of the cross."[2]

Moritz Lazarus, philosopher: "I am of the opinion that we should endeavor with all possible zeal to obtain an exact understanding of the great personality of Jesus and to reclaim him for Judaism."

Baruch Spinoza, one of the greatest of Jewish philosophers: "Christ was not so much a prophet as the mouthpiece of God. Christ was sent to teach not only Jews, but the whole human race; and therefore it was not enough that his mind should be accommodated to the opinions of the Jews alone, but also to the opinion and fundamental teaching common to the whole human race; in other words, to ideas universal and truth."[3]

Max Nordau, author and Zionist leader: "Jesus is the soul of our soul as he is the flesh of our flesh. Who then could think of excluding him from the people of Israel? St. Peter will remain the only Jew who said of the Son of David: 'I know not the man.' If the Jews up to the present have not rendered homage to the sublime beauty of the figure of Jesus, it is because their tormentors have always persecuted, tortured and assassinated in his name."[4]

Dr. Claude Montefiore, president of the Jewish Religious Union: "I cannot conceive that a time will come when the figure of Jesus will no longer be a star of the first magnitude in the spiritual heavens, when he will no longer be regarded as one of the greatest religious heroes and teachers the world has seen.... The religion of the future will be, as I believe, a developed and purified Judaism, but from that developed and purified Judaism the records will tell, however imperfectly, of perhaps its greatest teacher. Certainly its most potent and influential teacher will not be excluded."[5]

Hans Joachim Schoeps, Jewish theologian: "The church of Jesus Christ has preserved no portrait of its lord and saviour. If Jesus were to come again tomorrow, no Christian would know his face. But it might well be that he who is coming at the end of days, he who is awaited by the synagogue as by the church, is one, with one and the same face."[6]

Rabbi Emmanuel Weill: "Let us then as Jews be thankful there was a Jesus and a Paul. I do not know the secret of God, but I believe that Jesus and Christianity were providential means, useful to the Deity in guiding all men gradually and by an effort, keeping pace with the mental state of the majority of men, from paganism up to the pure and true idea of the divinity."[7]

Rabbi J.L. Levy: "I have little but contempt for those who cannot see in Jesus of Nazareth something to admire. I have little respect for those who cannot find in the Nazarene something good and worthy of our deep esteem. I personally regard him as one of the greatest spiritual teachers the world has ever known. I look upon him as one of the noblest spiritual teachers the human family has ever had the privilege of observing. We have great faith in the noble character of his life, in the beauty of his teaching that may safely be attributed to him. We have great admiration for the pure life offered for the good of humanity."

Rabbi H.G. Enelow, D.D., Reform Judaism rabbi, writer and scholar: "Among the great and the good that the human race has produced, none has ever approached Jesus in universality of appeal and sway. He has become the most fascinating figure in history. In him is combined what is best and most mysterious and most enchanting in Israel – the eternal people whose child he was. The Jew cannot help glorying in what he has meant to the world, nor can he help hoping that Jesus may yet serve as a bond of union between Jew and Christian."[8]

Rabbi David Phillipson, Ph.D., Reform Judaism leader: "There is no backwardness nor hesitancy on the part of modern Jewish thought in acknowledging the greatness of the teacher of Nazareth, the sweetness of his character, the power of his genius."[9]

Rabbi Gross of Brooklyn's Union Temple: "I, a rabbi of Israel, think we should accept Jesus. I think we should teach Jesus to children much as we teach them about Abraham, Moses and Jeremiah, and the rest of the great teachers and prophets. Jesus, as we all know, was a Jew. He was a gift of love."[10]

Rabbi Rudolph Grossman, D.D.: "We Jews honor the Nazarene as our brother in faith, sprung from our loins, nurtured at Israel's knee, a teacher of sweet and beautiful ideals, a preacher whose influence has been and still is among the mightiest spiritualizing factors in the world."[11]

Rabbi Gustav Gottheil, Ph.D., one of the founders of the Federation of American Zionists: "The keynote of prophetic religion of the Jewish prophets was holiness of life and purity of heart.... To place the Master of Nazareth by their side can surely be no dishonor to him, nor can it dim the luster of his name. If he has added to their spiritual bequests new jewels of religious truth, and spoken words which are words of life, because they touch the deepest springs of the human heart, why should we Jews not glorify in him?"[12]

Rabbi Maurice H. Harris: "Unlike the Messiahs before him – all mediocre men – his name (Jesus) has been treasured ever since as one of the great religious teachers of the world.... Let us not lose our Almighty Father in pantheistic vagueness, merging Him in nature; let us view Him as our Living redeemer, our Saviour, for we often need to be saved – sometimes from the world, sometimes from ourselves."[13]

Rabbi Stephen S. Wise, Ph.D., founder of the American Jewish Congress and the Federation of American Zionists: "Even if

Jesus had not been born unto Israel, even if he had borne no relation to the people of Israel, it becomes of importance for Israel to determine for itself what shall be its relation to the man who has touched the world nearly two thousand years as has no other single figure in history…. It is no mean joy and ignoble pride in us of the House of Israel to recognize, to honor and to cherish among our brothers – Jesus the Jew."[14]

CHAPTER 1:

How Jewish Scholars Answer the Question

"Who do you say that I am?"
This question echoes down through the ages and must be answered by every individual, both Jew and gentile.

How would you answer the question? Was Jesus merely a wise man, a good teacher? Or was he more? Was he a prophet who was sent by God? Or was he the one the Hebrew prophet Isaiah foretold – the Messiah who would be the sin-bearer for the people of Israel?

The following roundtable discussion recently took place within my mind. While the actual meeting was imaginary, the statements made by the Jewish scholars are quite genuine, as you will see by checking the footnotes. I'm sure that – like me, the Moderator – you'll find many of their comments surprising if not shocking. So let's listen in on the discussion, just now getting underway…

Moderator: Thank you all for being here. I know that with the exception of Benjamin Disraeli, none of you has expressed belief in Jesus as the Messiah. Since Mr. Disraeli *does* accept Jesus' claim to be the Messiah, I'd like to ask the distinguished Prime

Minister of England to make the first comment on the importance of Jesus.

Benjamin Disraeli: The pupil of Moses may ask himself whether all the princes of the House of David have done so much for the Jews as that Prince who was crucified.... Had it not been for him, the Jews would have been comparatively unknown or known only as a high Oriental Caste which had lost its country. Has not he made their history the most famous history in the world?[15]

Dr. Claude G. Montefiore, president of the Jewish Religious Union: We Jews do not mind saying that the greatest influence upon European and American history and civilization has been the Bible. But we too often forget that the Bible which has had this influence is not merely the Old Testament. It is the Old Testament and the New Testament combined. And of the two, it is the New Testament which has undoubtedly had the greater influence and has been of the greater importance.[16]

Moderator: That's all well and good, but what do you *personally* think of Jesus?

Dr. Montefiore: Jesus is the most important Jew that has ever lived, to whom the sinner and the outcast age after age have owed a great debt of gratitude.[17]

Moderator: And what is your opinion, Rabbi Enelow?

Rabbi H.G. Enelow, D.D., Reform Judaism rabbi and scholar: What does the modern Jew think of Jesus? A Prophet? Yes, crowning a great tradition, and who can compute all that Jesus has meant to humanity? The love he has inspired, the solace he has given, the good he has engendered, the hope and joy he has kindled – all that is unequaled in human history.[18]

Moderator: Rabbi Kohler, as president of Hebrew Union College, do you have anything to add?

Rabbi Kaufmann Kohler: No ethical system or religious catechism, however broad and pure, could equal the efficiency of this great personality, standing, unlike any other, midway between heaven and earth, equally near to God and to man.... Jesus, the helper of the poor, the friend of the sinner, the brother of every fellow-sufferer, the comforter of every sorrow-laden, the healer of the sick, the up-lifter of the fallen, the lover of man, the redeemer of woman, won the heart of mankind by storm. Jesus, the meekest of men, the most despised of the despised race of the Jews, mounted the world's throne to be the earth's Great King.[19]

Moderator: Those are strong words, rabbi. You say that Jesus is the earth's Great King. But what about his claim of being the Messiah, the one sent by God to die as a substitute for the sins of mankind? Anyone may answer.

Rabbi Solomon B. Freehof, Reform Judaism rabbi, scholar and author: Scores of men have believed themselves to be the Messiah and have convinced many of their contemporaries, but those who believed Jesus to be the Messiah have built a great church upon the rock of their belief. He is still the living comrade of countless lives. No Moslem ever sings, "Mohammed, lover of my soul", nor does any Jew say of Moses, the Teacher, "I need thee every hour."[20]

Moderator: Yes, Professor Rivkin, I see that you'd like to add something on this subject. For the benefit of our panelists who died long before he was born, Ellis Rivkin is professor of Jewish history at Hebrew Union College.

Ellis Rivkin: Of these Messianic claimants, only one, Jesus of Nazareth, so impressed his disciples that he became their Messiah. And he did so after the very crucifixion which should have refuted his claims decisively. But it was not Jesus' life which proved beyond question that he was the Messiah, the Christ. It was his resurrection.[21]

Moderator: That's a rather shocking statement, coming from a distinguished Jewish professor who doesn't believe in Jesus as Messiah. What then is your opinion of the theological significance of Jesus? Anyone? Yes, Mr. Schoeps.

Hans Joachim Schoeps, theologian and scholar of religious history: I would even go so far as to declare that perhaps no gentile can come to God the Father otherwise than through Jesus Christ…. The Christian who, according to his belief, comes to the Father through Jesus Christ ... stands before the same God in whom

CHAPTER 1: How Jewish Scholars Answer the Question

we Jews believe, the God of Abraham, of Isaac, and of Jacob, the God of Moses our teacher, to whom Jesus also said "Father."[22]

Moderator: Correct me if I'm wrong, but I don't think that any of you would consider Jesus to be a heretic. Am I right?

Pinchas E. Lapide, senior lecturer at Bar-Ilan University: I have the suspicion that Jesus was more loyal to the Torah than I am as an Orthodox Jew.[23]

Moderator: Professor Flusser, would you have anything to add to that?

David Flusser, professor of religious history at Hebrew University in Jerusalem: I do not think that many Jews would object if the Messiah – when he came – was the Jew Jesus.[24]

Moderator: That's a remarkable statement, professor! Since you and everyone else here seems to think so highly of Jesus, what should Jewish people today think about Jesus? Is it a sin for a Jew to take a close look at Jesus?

Dr. Chaim Zhitlowsky, Jewish scholar and author: Every Jew should be proud of the fact that Jesus is our brother, flesh of our flesh and blood of our blood. We desire to put him back where he belongs.[25]

Moderator: And where exactly *does* Jesus belong in the minds and hearts of Jewish people?

Constantine Brunner, Jewish philosopher: What is this? Is it only the Jew who is unable to see and hear? Are the Jews stricken with blindness and deafness as regards Christ, so that to them only he has nothing to say? Is he to be of no importance to us Jews?[26]

Moderator: What exactly are you getting at?

Brunner: Understand then what we shall do. We shall bring him back to us. Christ is not dead for us – for us he has not yet lived; and he will not slay us, he will make us live again. His profound and holy words, and all that is true and heart-appealing in the New Testament, must from now on be heard in our synagogues and taught to our children, in order that the wrong we had committed may be made good, the curse turned into a blessing, and that he at last may find us who has always been seeking after us.[27]

Who Do You Say That I Am?

Moderator: Remarkable words, Mr. Brunner. I'd like to go on but I'm afraid we've run out of time. My thanks to all of you for joining us today. For next time, I have asked eight respected Jewish authors to join us as we look at Jesus' question: "Who do you say that I am?" Until then, I will leave you – and our readers – with one final question: If Jesus was not the Messiah, can you think of any person in history who better fits the description given by Moses, David and the Jewish prophets? As all of you know, there are several hundred Messianic prophecies in the Torah, the prophets and the writings. Let me quickly mention a few:

According to the Hebrew prophets, the Messiah would be born of a virgin (Isaiah 7:14) in the town of Bethlehem (Micah 5:2). He would be preceded by a forerunner (Malachi 3:1) and would arrive before the destruction of the Temple – which occurred approximately 40 years after the crucifixion of Jesus (Daniel 9:24-26). Furthermore, the Messiah would be a prophet like Moses (Deuteronomy 18:18-19), rejected by his own people (Isaiah 53:3), betrayed by a friend (Psalm 41:9), sold for 30 pieces of silver (Zechariah 11:12), smitten, spat upon and mocked (Psalm 22:7-8) and finally crucified (Psalm 22). His death would be considered a sacrifice, for the Messiah would bear the sins of the people (Isaiah 53). The prophets also predicted that the Messiah would be buried among the wealthy (Isaiah 53:9), but the grave would not hold him (Psalm 16:10).

The most revealing Messianic portrait of the entire Old Testament, however, is found in the 53rd chapter of Isaiah.

CHAPTER 1: How Jewish Scholars Answer the Question

Isaiah 53

1 Who hath believed our report? And to whom is the arm of the LORD revealed?

2 For he shall grow up before him like a tender plant, and like a root out of a dry ground; he hath no form nor comeliness, and when we shall see him, there is no beauty that we should desire him.

3 He is despised and rejected of men, a man of sorrows, and acquainted with grief, and we hid as it were our faces from him; he was despised, and we esteemed him not.

4 Surely he hath borne our griefs, and carried our sorrows; yet we did esteem him stricken, smitten of God, and afflicted.

5 But he was wounded for our transgressions, he was bruised for our iniquities; the chastisement for our peace was upon him, and with his stripes we are healed.

6 All we like sheep have gone astray; we have turned every one to his own way, and the LORD hath laid on him the iniquity of us all.

7 He was oppressed, and he was afflicted, yet he opened not his mouth; he is brought as a lamb to the slaughter, and as a sheep before her shearers is dumb, so he openeth not his mouth.

8 He was taken from prison and from judgment; and who shall declare his generation? For he was cut off out of the land of the living; for the transgression of my people was he stricken.

9 And he made his grave with the wicked, and with the rich in his death, because he had done no violence, neither was any deceit in his mouth.

10 Yet it pleased the LORD to bruise him; he hath put him to grief. When thou shalt make his soul an offering for sin, he shall see his seed, he shall prolong his days, and the pleasure of the LORD shall prosper in his hand.

11 He shall see of the travail of his soul, and shall be satisfied; by his knowledge shall my righteous servant justify many; for he shall bear their iniquities.

12 Therefore will I divide him a portion with the great, and he shall divide the spoil with the strong, because he hath poured out his soul unto death: and he was numbered with the transgressors; and he bore the sin of many, and made intercession for the transgressors.

This prophetic portrait of a suffering Messiah, written some 700 years before the birth of Jesus, is never read aloud in synagogue. Interestingly, the 52nd and 54th chapters of Isaiah are read aloud each year in the synagogue's haftorah readings, but the 53rd chapter is skipped.

Was the omission of the 53rd chapter a mere coincidence or was it deliberate? Here's what Herbert Loewe, Reader in Rabbinics at Cambridge University, wrote:

"Because of the christological interpretation given to the chapter by Christians, it is omitted from the series of prophetical lessons (Haftarot) for the Deuteronomy Sabbaths.... The omission is deliberate and striking."[28]

Could it be that the 53rd chapter of Isaiah is omitted because Isaiah's description of the Messiah bears such a striking resemblance to Jesus of Nazareth? I'll leave that for the reader to decide.

CHAPTER 1: How Jewish Scholars Answer the Question

CHAPTER 2:

How Jewish Authors Answer the Question

"Who do you say that I am?"

No question has ever caused such controversy as this one. According to Christians – who base their thinking on a Bible consisting of both Old and New Testaments – your answer to this crucial question decides your eternal destiny.

To see how some notable Jewish people would answer the question, I recently convened a second roundtable discussion to which I invited eight famous Jewish authors. All of the panelists showed up right on time, which came as no surprise since the discussion took place within the confines of my own mind. This does not mean, however, that I dreamed up their statements. All of the quotes are footnoted for the benefit of readers who want to make certain that the quotes are real and have not been taken out of context.

With that introduction out of the way, pull up a chair and listen to what these great Jewish authors had to say about Jesus.

CHAPTER 2: How Jewish Authors Answer the Question

Moderator: Gentlemen, thank you all for being here today. I know you're all very busy, so I'll get right to my first question: Does anyone here believe that Jewish people have anything to gain by taking a closer look at the life of Jesus of Nazareth?

Israel Zangwill: We shall never get the future straight until we disentangle the past. To disentangle the past means to re-examine the trial of Jesus – myths woven purposely by our leaders around the greatest and most notable personality in history, only that we may not see and recognize the real Jesus. To us, my brethren, in this our day, is given the privilege to reclaim the Christ we have lost for so many centuries.[29]

Moderator: And who is this "real Jesus" you're talking about?

Zangwill: Has not the crucified Christ more than fulfilled the highest and noblest of our greatest prophets? Is not he the incarnation of the essence of what the Law, the Psalms and the Prophets taught?[30]

Moderator: But most rabbis say that only ignorant Jews or those who have been deceived by others would turn to Jesus. Isn't this what you believe also?

Max Brod: I am constantly amazed at the naiveté of our teachers and leaders who are surprised when I tell them that the best of our youth, our intellectuals, become Christians out of conviction…. Our "leaders" do not believe it. To them, a Jew never becomes a Christian unless he wants to better his position. That Christianity has drawn to itself such noble souls as Pascal, Novalis, Kirkegaard, Amiel, Dostoyevsky, Claudel, etc., etc., and that it exercises a most overwhelming influence on the most earnest truth-seekers among us, of that our teachers know nothing.[31]

Moderator: According to some polls, there are now well over a hundred thousand Jewish followers of Jesus throughout the world. Is there an upsurge in Jews turning to Jesus or am I imagining things?

Gustav Lazlo: The movement for the recognition of Christ by the Jews is not a fantasy arising from (my) brain. In the hearts and minds of many men, ordinary men like myself, traders, men of affairs, the fact that Christ is the only leader who can take us anywhere worth going to is coming to new recognition.[32]

Moderator: I'd like to read you something from the pen of a great Jewish historian and Bible scholar who couldn't be here with us today. Speaking of Jesus, Heinrich Graetz said, and I quote, "He felt within himself the call to save the lost sheep of the house of Israel.... He, by word and example, raised the sinner and the publican, and filled the hearts of those poor, neglected, thoughtless beings with the love of God, transforming them into dutiful children of their Heavenly Father. He animated them with his own piety and fervor, and improved their conduct by the hope he gave them of being able to enter the kingdom of heaven."[33]

Let me ask, do any of you share this historian's lofty view of Jesus?

Ernest R. Trattner: No Jewish prophet before Jesus ever searched out the miserable, the sick, the weak, and the downtrodden in order to pour forth love and compassionate service. He went out of his way to redeem the lowly by a touch of human sympathy that is altogether unique in Jewish history.[34]

Moderator: Sholem Asch, you've written novels about Jesus. What are your views?

Sholem Asch: Jesus Christ, to me, is the outstanding personality of all time, of all history, both as Son of God and as Son of Man. Everything he ever said or did has value for us today, and that is something you can say of no other man, alive or dead.... Every act and word of Jesus has value for all of us, wherever we are. He became the Light of the World. Why shouldn't I, a Jew, be proud of that? No other religious leader, either, has ever become so personal a part of people as the Nazarene. When you understand Jesus, you understand that he came to save you, to come into your personality. It isn't just a case of a misty, uncertain relationship between a worshiper and an unseen God. That is abstract; Jesus is personal.[35]

Moderator: Dr. Singer, as managing editor of *The Jewish Encyclopedia*, do you share any of Mr. Asch's opinions?

Isidore Singer, Ph.D.: I regard Jesus of Nazareth as a Jew of Jews, one whom all Jewish people are learning to love. His teachings have been an immense service to the world in bringing Israel's God to the knowledge of hundreds of millions of mankind.... We are all glad to claim Jesus as one of our people.[36]

Moderator: Mr. Weinstock, as an author and labor leader, you come from a very different background than Dr. Singer. Do you agree that Jesus performed a valuable service by bringing Israel's God to the knowledge of millions throughout the world?

Harris Weinstock: Without Jesus and without Paul, the God of Israel would still have been the God of a handful, the God of a petty, obscure and insignificant tribe. Let the Jew, despite the centuries of persecution and suffering, be thankful that there was a Jesus and a Paul. Let him more fully appreciate that through the wonderful influence of these heroic characters the mission of the Jew is being fulfilled, and his teachings are being spread to the remotest nooks and corners of the world by Christianity.[37]

Moderator: One of us, I notice, has been silent throughout this discussion. And yet I believe he is the most qualified to make a comment, since he was born just a few years after the time of Jesus. I am speaking, of course, about Flavius Josephus, the illustrious Jewish author, historian and general of the Galilean Jewish army in the war against Rome. Mr. Josephus, although some skeptics today claim you never actually wrote about Jesus, I'd like you to read the paragraph that appears in all of the most ancient manuscripts of your *Antiquities of the Jews*. I'm sure you know which paragraph I'm talking about, so go right ahead.

Flavius Josephus: Now there was about this time Jesus, a wise man, if it be lawful to call him a man, for he was a doer of wonderful works, a teacher of such men as receive the truth with pleasure. He drew over to him both many of the Jews, and many of the Gentiles. He was the Christ, and when Pilate, at the suggestion of the principal men among us, had condemned him to the cross, those that loved him at the first did not forsake him, for he appeared to them alive again the third day; as the divine prophets had foretold these and ten thousand other wonderful things concerning him. And the tribe of Christians, so named from him, are not extinct at this day.[38]

Moderator: Not at the present day either, Mr. Josephus. I think your comments have special significance to those who question the accuracy of the New Testament. Since you were born in the year 37 C.E. – just a few years after the death of Jesus – you were able to talk with actual eyewitnesses of the events. Thank you – and thanks to each one of you – for being with us here today.

If the quote is authentic – and we believe that it is – Josephus called Jesus "the Christ" which is a translation of the term "Messiah." There can be no doubt, however, that over the past twenty centuries, many hundreds of thousands of Jews have come to agree with Simon ben Jonah that Jesus was and is "the Messiah, the Son of the living God."

Now, what is *your* response to Jesus' question? But before you answer, consider seriously the words of Israel Zangwill: "To us, my brethren, in this our day, is given the privilege to reclaim the Christ we have lost for so many centuries."

CHAPTER 2: How Jewish Authors Answer the Question

CHAPTER 3:

How Will You Answer the Question?

"Who do you say that I am?"
When Jesus asked that question, one of his closest followers, a Jewish man, replied, "You are the Messiah, the Son of the Living God."

Jesus responded, "Blessed are you, Simon son of Jonah, for this was not revealed to you by man, but by my Father in heaven."

Clearly, Jesus accepted the titles "Messiah" and "Son of the Living God." Now, what did that mean to Jesus and to those who heard him? Two thousand years ago, the Jewish people understood "Son of God" to mean "of the same substance as God" or "equal to God." That's why the Jewish people said to Pontius Pilate, procurator of Judaea, "We have a law, and by that law he (Jesus) ought to die, because he made himself the Son of God" (John 19:7).

Jesus clearly claimed equality with God. In fact, during the Feast of Chanukah, Jesus told a crowd of Jewish people, "I and my Father are one." The historical record says that the crowd took up stones to put him to death on the spot. Why? In their own words,

CHAPTER 3: How Will You Answer the Question?

"For a good work we stone thee not; but for blasphemy; and because that thou, being a man, makest thyself God" (John 10:33).

So let's dismiss at the outset the notion, held by a few today, that Jesus never claimed to be equal with God. The Jewish people of Jesus' day understood an important fact that is often evaded today: Jesus was absolutely sure that he was God!

Take a look for a moment at a few of his many claims.

- He claimed authority to tell people their sins were forgiven, thus exercising a right that belongs only to God (Mark 2:5-11).
- He claimed to be without sin, thus contrasting himself with the rest of mankind (John 8:46).
- He claimed that the only way anyone could truly know the Father was by knowing him (John 14:6).
- He claimed God-like power when he said, "I am the resurrection and the life; he that believeth in me, though he were dead, yet shall he live" (John 11:25).
- He claimed for himself titles and names reserved for God alone (John 8:58).

Without any shadow of doubt, Jesus claimed to be God's equal.

Now, what do we do today with a man who claims to be God? Do we call him "a good man" or "a wonderful teacher"? Obviously not ... and yet that is precisely what most rabbis today say about Jesus.

For instance, as we saw earlier, Rabbi J.L. Levy looks at Jesus and says, "I personally regard him as one of the greatest spiritual teachers the world has ever known."

Reform Judaism leader Rabbi David Philipson acknowledges "the greatness of the teacher of Nazareth, the sweetness of his character, the power of his genius."

Rabbi Rudolph Grossman, D.D., concurs: "We Jews honor the Nazarene as our brother in faith, sprung from our loins, nurtured at Israel's knee, a teacher of sweet and beautiful ideals, a preacher whose influence has been and still is among the mightiest spiritualizing factors in the world."

On and on it goes. Jesus – one who claimed to be God – is described by rabbis as a spiritual teacher, a genius, a preacher, a teacher of beautiful ideals. But what they have all failed to realize is that if Jesus was not God, then he was not a good person.

C.S. Lewis, formerly professor at Cambridge University and a one-time agnostic, understood the inconsistency of this thinking quite well. In his book *Mere Christianity*, Lewis wrote:

"I am trying here to prevent anyone saying the really foolish thing that people often say about Him: 'I'm ready to accept Jesus as a great moral teacher, but I don't accept His claim to be God.' This is the one thing we must not say. A man who was merely a man and said the sort of things Jesus said would not be a great moral teacher. He would either be a lunatic – on a level with the man who says he is a poached egg – or else he would be the Devil of Hell. You must make your choice. Either this man was, and is, the Son of God: or else a madman or something worse. You can shut Him up for a fool, you can spit at Him and kill Him as a demon; or you can fall at His feet and call Him Lord and God. But let us not come up with any patronizing nonsense about His being a great human teacher. He has not left that open to us. He did not intend to."[39]

So if what Lewis wrote is correct – if Jesus cannot be considered merely a wise teacher of spiritual ideals – what options are open to us?

There are four options and four alone:
1. *Lunatic* – Jesus was deluded.
2. *Liar* – Jesus was a deceiver.
3. *Legend* – Jesus' followers made him into God.
4. *Lord* – Jesus was who he claimed to be: equal with the Lord God of Israel.

Let's briefly examine each one in turn.

The Lunatic Option

If Jesus truly thought that he was God – but in reality was not – then he must have been deluded, insane. Is this an option we Jews should take seriously?

The thought that Jesus was insane runs counter to the mainstream of Jewish opinion. For example, Dr. Claude Montefiore, president of the Jewish Religious Union, said, "Jesus is the most important Jew that has ever lived, to whom the sinner and the outcast age after age, have owed a great debt of gratitude."[40]

Baruch Spinoza, one of our greatest Jewish philosophers, said, "Christ was sent to teach not only Jews, but the whole human race; and therefore it was not enough that his mind should be accommodated to the opinions of the Jews alone, but also to the opinion and fundamental teaching common to the whole human race; in other words, to ideas universal and truth."[41]

No one can read the New Testament without being struck by the calmness and self-possession of its main character. When everything around him was in turmoil, Jesus exercised the self-control of a well-balanced person who was very much in touch with reality.

Turning once again to C.S. Lewis, "The discrepancy between the depth and sanity ... of his moral teaching and the rampant megalomania which must lie behind His theological teaching unless He is indeed God, has never been satisfactorily got over."[42]

No, Jesus of Nazareth was certainly no raving lunatic ... and few rabbis or Jewish thinkers have ever thought to call him that.

The Liar Option

If Jesus knew that he wasn't God – but repeatedly told people that he was – then he was a despicable liar. Not only that, if Jesus was a liar, then he was also a fool, because he paid for his deceptive words with his life.

In fact, we can also call Jesus a hypocrite, because he told others to be honest, whatever the cost, while telling the most colossal lie of all time.

Was Jesus, then, a liar, a fool, a hypocrite?

Reform Judaism Rabbi H.G. Enelow didn't think so. He called Jesus a prophet, crowning a great tradition. "Who can compute all that Jesus has meant to humanity? The love he has inspired, the solace he has given, the good he has engendered, the hope and joy he has kindled – all that is unequaled in human history."[43]

Constantine Brunner, the great Jewish philosopher, didn't think so either: "His profound and holy words, and all that is true and heart-appealing in the New Testament, must from now on be heard in our synagogues and taught to our children."[44]

The Jewish historian Dr. J.M. Jost wasn't portraying a despicable liar or hypocrite when he described Jesus with these words: "Spotless walk, unselfish love for mankind. Thousands of Jews adored Jesus, their teacher and friend."[45]

It is simply inconceivable that a man who taught the things that Jesus taught and lived the life that Jesus lived could have been such a monstrous liar. The consensus of Jewish thought has never considered the liar option as viable.

The Legend Option

Perhaps, then, Jesus never really claimed to be God? Maybe it was his followers who made him into God through their writings? This is the "legend hypothesis" – and this, too, has been disproved by historians, Bible scholars, archaeologists and experts in the discipline of legal evidence.

Of great importance is the fact that with the exception of John, all of those who recorded the history of Jesus were martyred for their beliefs. They could have lived their lives free from torture and persecution had they denied the truth of their writings. But they all chose to die painful deaths rather than deny the facts that they had recorded.

Judges and experts in legal testimony agree that their willingness to die constitutes unshakable evidence that the writers truly believed what they wrote. According to legal experts, people might lay down their lives for a lie which they sincerely believe, but they *won't* die for a lie of their own making.

CHAPTER 3: How Will You Answer the Question?

Secondly, in order for a legend to develop, one essential element is required – time. A great deal of time must pass before a legend can take hold. For example, if we wanted to fabricate a legend today that John F. Kennedy claimed to be God and that he was raised from the dead three days after he was shot, no one would believe our story. Why? Because not enough time has passed. There are simply too many people alive today who would say that our story was nonsense.

Time – the essential ingredient for cooking up a legend – is something that the writers of the New Testament simply did not have. They had completed their writing while actual eyewitnesses of the events were still alive.

Those today who want to believe in the legend hypothesis have tried to make it appear that the New Testament was written two or more generations after the events it describes. This, they believe, would be time enough for a legend to arise. However, the most painstaking biblical scholarship and the spade of the archaeologist won't let them get away with such a late date of authorship.

According to William F. Albright, considered to be the world's foremost biblical archaeologist:

"We can already say emphatically that there is no longer any solid basis for dating any book of the New Testament after about A.D. 80, two full generations before the date between 130-150 given by the more radical New Testament critics of today. In my opinion, every book of the New Testament was written by a baptized Jew between the forties and the eighties of the first century A.D."[46]

Even if we accept a date as late as 95 A.D. for the completion of the New Testament, there still was not enough time to have successfully tricked the world into believing such a monumental legend. Some eyewitnesses would still have been alive.

Moreover, no opponent of Jesus and no secular writers who lived at that time even suggested that Jesus' miracles or his resurrection didn't actually take place.

Jewish authorities today are coming to believe in the essential historicity of the New Testament. That's why it is even being taught in a growing number of yeshivas and Jewish centers of learning throughout the world.

Not even clear-thinking Jewish scientists accept the legend hypothesis. When the *Saturday Evening Post* asked Albert Einstein if he accepted the historical existence of Jesus, he responded, "Unquestionably! No one can read the Gospels without feeling the actual presence of Jesus. His personality pulsates in every word. No myth is filled with such life."[47]

We also must remember that it simply would not have been possible for anyone to have created a Jesus. Historian Philip Schaff tells us why:

"A character so original, so complete, so uniformly consistent, so perfect, so human and yet so high above all human greatness, can be neither a fraud nor a fiction. The poet, as has been well said, would in this case be greater than the hero. It would take more than a Jesus to invent a Jesus."[48]

The Only Option that Remains

If you dismiss the first three options, the only option left is that Jesus was exactly who he said he was – the Messiah.

While there have been many pretenders to the Messianic throne, only one – Jesus of Nazareth – was able to support his claims by fulfilling the Messianic prophecies of the ancient Jewish Scriptures.

We've already taken a look at a handful of prophecies Jesus fulfilled. In all, Jesus fulfilled more than 300 Old Testament prophecies, as it has been well documented by historians and scholars. But the most convincing proof of his Messiahship was his resurrection. We repeat what Ellis Rivkin, professor of Jewish history at Hebrew Union College, has said about the resurrection of Jesus:

"Of these Messianic claimants, only one, Jesus of Nazareth, so impressed His disciples that He became their Messiah. And He did so after the very crucifixion which should have refuted His claims decisively. But it was not Jesus' life which proved beyond question that He was the Messiah, the Christ. It was His resurrection."[49]

CHAPTER 3: How Will You Answer the Question?

Rabbi Pinchas Lapide – an Orthodox Jew, theologian and specialist in New Testament studies – wrote in his book *The Resurrection of Jesus: a Jewish Perspective* – "I accept the resurrection of Jesus not as an invention of the community of disciples, but as a historical event." [50]

According to Rabbi Lapide: "When this scared, frightened band of apostles which was just about to throw away everything in order to flee in despair to Galilee; when these peasants, shepherds, and fishermen, who betrayed and denied their master and failed him so miserably, suddenly could be changed overnight into a confident mission society, convinced of salvation and able to work with much more success after Easter than before, then no vision or hallucination is sufficient to explain such a revolutionary transformation." [51]

Recognizing that Jesus fulfilled the hundreds of prophecies from the Jewish Scriptures – and believing that he will fulfill the remaining prophecies upon his return – multitudes of Jews and gentiles, from the first century to the present day, have called Jesus "Lord, Messiah, the Son of God, the Holy One of Israel."

Now Jesus of Nazareth turns to you and asks:

"Who do you say that I am?"

FOOTNOTES

[1] *Jesus of Nazareth*, The Macmillan Co., 1925.
[2] *History of the Jews*, Volume II.
[3] *Tractatus Theologica-Politicus*.
[4] Quoted in *Unto His Own* by Dr. Jacob Gartenhaus. Marshall, Morgan and Scott Publishers.
[5] Gartenhaus, op.cit.
[6] "A Religious Bridge Between Jew and Christian", *Commentary*, February 1950.
[7] Gartenhaus, op.cit.
[8] Ibid.
[9] Cited frequently in the literature and on the Internet. Original citation unknown.
[10] Ibid.
[11] Ibid.
[12] Ibid.
[13] Ibid.
[14] *The Outlook*, June 7, 1913.
[15] Gartenhaus, op.cit.
[16] Quoted by D.B. Bravin, *The Dawn*, Sept-Oct 1932.
[17] *Jewish Chronicle*, July 14, 1909.

[18] Quoted from *The New Jews* by James C. Hefley, Tyndale House.

[19] Address before the Congress in 1893, quoted by Jacob Jocz in *The Jewish People and Jesus Christ*, Baker Book House.

[20] *Stormers of Heaven* by Rabbi Solomon B. Freehof, Harper & Brothers.

[21] Quoted from "The Meaning of Messiah in Jewish Thought" by Ellis Rivkin, *Evangelicals and Jews in Conversation*, Baker Book House.

[22] "A Religious Bridge Between Jew and Christian," *Commentary*, Feb. 1950.

[23] Quoted in *Time*, Apr. 18, 1977.

[24] Ibid.

[25] *Das Neue Leben* by Dr. Chaim Zhitlowsky, as quoted in *Unto His Own* by Dr. Jacob Gartenhaus, Marshall, Morgan and Scott Publishers.

[26] *Der Juden Hass und die Juden* by Constantine Brunner (pen name of Leopold Wertheimer), quoted in The Rebirth of the State of Israel by Dr. Arthur W. Kac, Baker Book House.

[27] Ibid.

[28] Montefiore, C. and Loewe, H. *A Rabbinic Anthology*, Schocken Books, p. 544.

[29] Gartenhaus, op.cit.

[30] Ibid.

[31] Quoted by D.B. Bravin, *The Dawn*, Jan-Feb 1934.

[32] From a letter written to the *Morning Post* (London) as quoted in *The Rebirth of the State of Israel* by Dr. Arthur W. Kac, Baker Book House.

[33] Quoted in *The Eternal God Revealing Himself* by David L. Cooper, Ph.D., The Evangelical Press.

[34] Trattner, Ernest R., *As A Jew Sees Jesus*, Charles Scribner's Sons.

[35] Mead, Frank S., "An Interview with Sholem Asch", an article printed in *Christian Herald*, January 1944.

[36] Cooper, David L. op.cit.

[37] Weinstock, Harris, *Jesus the Jew*, Funk & Wagnalls Co.

[38] Josephus, Flavius, *The Antiquities of the Jews*, xviii.33.

[39] Lewis, C.S., *Mere Christianity*, Macmillan Company, pp. 55-56.

[40] *Jewish Chronicle*, July 14, 1909.

[41] *Tractatus Theologica-Politicus.*

[42] Lewis, C.S., *Miracles: A Preliminary Study*, Macmillan Company, p. 113.

[43] Enelow, Hyman G, *A Jewish View of Jesus*, Macmillan Company, p. 181.

[44] Brunner, Constantine, op.cit., p. 34.

[45] Jost, J.M. *The History of Judaism and Their Sects*, Vol. 1, Chap. 12.

[46] Albright, W.F., *Recent Discoveries in Bible Lands*, Funk & Wagnalls Co. Also quoted in Christianity Today, Jan. 1963.

[47] Viereck, George S. "What Life Means to Einstein," *Saturday Evening Post*, Oct. 26, 1929.

[48] Schaff, Philip. History of the Christian Church, Wm B. Eerdmans Publishing Co.

[49] Quoted from "The Meaning of Messiah in Jewish Thought" by Ellis Rivkin, *Evangelicals and Jews in Conversation*, Baker Book House, p. 62.

[50] Lapide, Pinchas. *The Resurrection of Jesus: a Jewish Perspective.* Wipf & Stock Publishers, 2002.

[51] Ibid.

BONUS RELEASE:

Dear Rabbi, Tell Me About Jesus

A Series of Letters Between a Hebrew-Christian and a Conservative Jewish Rabbi

by
Steve Schwartz

©1976-2009, Steve Schwartz.
All Rights Reserved.

INTRODUCTION

"Come now, and let us reason together," says the Lord. Though your sins are as scarlet, they will be as white as snow; though they are red like crimson, they will be like wool." (Isaiah 1:18)

This verse from the Hebrew prophet Isaiah has meant much to me. It reveals that God wants to *reason* with us. He doesn't expect us to take a blind leap of faith into unreality or non-reason. He gives us credit for being intelligent, reasoning creatures, and He desires to communicate certain truths to us in His written word, the Bible.

Upon hearing that someone was a "Bible-believer," I used to think: "How can a person of such intelligence accept such foolishness?" But that was before I studied the Bible for myself. In 1975 I found out for myself what it was like to be a Bible-believer, and I discovered that it was more intellectually, emotionally and spiritually satisfying than anything else I had ever experienced. It required faith but not a blind leap of faith.

To the contrary, before I accepted the Bible as God's truth, I first investigated both sides, devouring books by both the skeptic and the believer. I read books on history, archaeology, theology and philosophy. I studied the Bible, the Talmud, and many Jewish and

Christian writings. I didn't begin my studies in an objective manner; I was a non-believer through-and-through.

But when my preconceptions started to crumble under the weight of facts, I had no other choice but to accept the Word of God without reservation. Of course, this meant that my new belief was bound to be at odds with modern Jewish thought. especially as it concerns the Messiah.

Naturally, I had many questions which I felt could best be answered by a rabbi. The material you see here consists of correspondence between myself and a Conservative Jewish rabbi who is head of a large congregation in the Midwest.

It is my sincere hope that you read the letters with an open mind and an honest desire to discover the truth. Weigh both sides of the debate and then make up your own mind.

Letter #1

My First Letter to the Rabbi

Dear Rabbi,

It's been a long time, rabbi. I don't know if you'll even remember me. I'm happy to report that my wife and I are doing fine, and we are the proud parents of a baby girl. We named her Rebecca after the wife of Isaac, the Old Testament patriarch.

Speaking of the Old Testament, I have been studying it intensively for the past two years, and I've found many remarkable things in it. I have many questions that I'd like to ask you, rabbi, which is really the primary reason I am writing you at this time. I'd like to hear how you would answer the following questions.

1. According to the 70 rabbis who worked on the Septuagint translation of the Old Testament, the Hebrew word "almah" (Isaiah 7:14) is translated "parthenos" meaning virgin. Why do the rabbis today say it means "young woman"? Are they simply trying to dispose of the argument for the virgin birth of Christ?

2. I'm sure you know the meaning of the two words "yachid" and "echad" for *one*. Why is the word "echad" (meaning a *composite* oneness) used to describe God in the *Shema* while Moses Maimonides uses "yachid" (meaning *absolute* oneness) in his Thirteen Articles of Faith? Is Maimonides trying to dispose of Old Testament evidence in support of the triunity of God?

3. Why are the 52nd and 54th chapters of Isaiah read aloud every year in the synagogue, but Isaiah 53 is *never* read? This chapter seems to describe the life, trial, death and resurrection of Jesus. Is this why the chapter is skipped?

Furthermore, if the Suffering Servant of this chapter is "Israel", as the rabbis today claim, how can the servant die as a substitute for the sins of Isaiah's people – Israel? That would mean that Israel is dying as a *substitute* for the sins of Israel ... which doesn't make any sense.

4. Whose death is described by David in the 22nd Psalm? Also, how could David describe death by crucifixion when that manner of capital punishment was unknown at the time? I know that Christians believe this psalm predicts the sufferings and death of Jesus.

5. The Old Testament (particularly Leviticus) testifies that there is no atonement without blood, sacrificed on the altar. Where do we get the idea that our sins are forgiven by going without food or water for a 24-hour period? It seems to me that God is pretty specific ... and He never lifted His requirement for the atoning blood. It seems to me that today we have a Day of Atonement ... but no atonement.

6. Finally, the Old Testament says that the Messiah would be a descendant of Abraham through Isaac through Jacob through Judah, of the house of David, that he would be born of a virgin (Isaiah 7:14) in the town of Bethlehem (Micah 5:2), that he would be preceded by a forerunner (Malachi 3:1), and it even predicts that he would arrive before the destruction of the Temple – which occurred in the year 70 C.E. (Daniel 9:24-26).

Furthermore, the Messiah would be a prophet like Moses (Deuteronomy 18:18-19), rejected by his own people (Isaiah 53:3), betrayed by a friend (Psalm 41:9), sold for thirty pieces of silver (Zechariah 11:12), smitten, spat upon and mocked (Psalm 22:7-8), crucified (Psalm 22), but would be raised from the dead in three days (Psalm 16:10, Jonah 1:17).

There are more than 300 prophecies in the Old Testament which all find their fulfillment in one particular man ... and you know which man I'm speaking about. Now, who do *you* say the prophets are speaking about?

7. Permit me one more question, rabbi. Who is Jesus of Nazareth? I know you don't think that he is God, and that's certainly what I believed; but who, then, is he? If he is not God, then he must be either a lunatic (who really believed he was the Messiah) or a liar who was despicable enough to draw people away from God.

From the staggering things he said about himself, it doesn't seem possible to dismiss him simply as a good or wise man. My final question is, Who is Jesus Christ: lunatic, liar or Lord?

I know these aren't easy questions for you to answer, but I would greatly appreciate hearing from you as soon as you have the time.

Incidentally, I happen to believe – like the great Jewish philosophers and theologians – that the Old Testament is the actual Word of God, so I hope you'll use Moses and the prophets as your authority.

Thank you for your help, rabbi, and I'll look forward to hearing from you.

Sincerely,
Steve Schwartz

Dear Rabbi

Letter #2

The Rabbi's Response

Dear Steve,

It was really a wonderful surprise to hear from you. I do remember you, and I'm glad to hear that you and Carol are happy and that your Rebecca Is a wonderful young lady. May she grow in health and peace.

I'm most happy to answer your questions. However, I would suggest that you try to get either of two books from the public library. The first is entitled A Jewish Understanding of the New Testament by Samuel Sandmel. The second is by the same author, entitled We Jews and You Christians.

If you cannot find them either at the library or at the local synagogue, please let me know and I will try to find them for you. They are by a professor who is considered the leading Jewish expert on early Christianity and the New Testament.

I now hasten to answer your seven questions as quickly as possible.

1. The Hebrew word, "almah" is recognized by 99% of Biblical scholars today as meaning young woman. The translation of the Septuagint into "parthenos" is accepted even by most Christian scholars as a misinterpretation.

That is why such versions of the Bible as the Revised Standard Version and the New English Bible – both published by Protestant groups – translate the virgin as "young woman." It did not mean only a virgin, although a young woman of that age could be a virgin.

The question, Steve, is whether you are going to read something into the Biblical story or to accept it as it is. In its context, Isaiah is merely telling the king that before this young woman gives birth, the two kings to the north will be destroyed.

I believe in reading the Bible for what it contains, not reading a later thought into it.

2. The two words "yachid" and "echad" actually mean the same thing. Maimonides uses "yachid" which was the popular form of the Hebrew during the Middle Ages. Just as Old English of the Middle Ages is different from Modern English, so the Biblical Hebrew was slightly different from the medieval Hebrew.

However, there is absolutely no difference between the words one and unity. As a matter of fact, they are based on the same three Hebrew letters. Once again, to read in the idea of "composite oneness" distorts the meaning of the original Hebrew.

3. It is not true that the 53rd chapter of the Book of Isaiah is never read. All of the section known as "Suffering Servant" is read during the synagogue year. We Jews have taken the "Suffering Servant" to be a symbol of the Jewish people.

All Jews are suffering servants and all serve to purify God through their suffering. When you say that the "Suffering Servant" is Israel, I think that you are misinterpreting this to mean the State of Israel. Israel in this context means the children of Israel, the people of Israel, the Jewish people.

Many Jews have died and suffered not only for our sins but for the sins of the Christians and Moslems who inflicted death upon us.

4. David's Psalm 22 describes the "Prayer of a Lonely Soul." Never once is crucifixion mentioned in David's Psalm. Again, Steve, why read things into the Bible that are not there? May I suggest that you go to the library and get a copy of "The Interpreter's Bible," Volume 4. Beginning on page 115, you will see commentaries on the Psalm.

Certainly, Jesus, having been a Jew, knowing this verse, quoted it when on the cross. But because he did doesn't mean that David was crucified. This was merely the prayer of one who was very lonely and upset.

5. The Bible does say that sacrifices are necessary. However, the Talmud tells us that after the destruction of the Temple by the Romans in the year 70 of this Era, sacrifices were replaced by prayer, good deeds and charity. In this way, the Jew not only atones for his sins, but acts in a way to bring praise to himself and God.

Yom Kippur is one day out of the year that we remember about our sins. However, our atonement goes on forever. We are told that we cannot pray to God for forgiveness unless we first ask our fellowman for forgiveness. Atonement must be a very personal thing, and we Jews atone directly to God rather than through an intermediary or a middle-man.

6. I can understand your feelings by pulling a verse here and a verse there about the Messiah. However, you have to understand that many of these sections of the Bible were written hundreds of years apart. It would be easy for me to pull verses from any book after I have a belief in a certain man as Messiah, and say that they proved it.

It is impossible to answer your question in a short paragraph. You have to know all about the Bible, about Jewish history, and about each of the authors and the contexts of their statements to understand it.

May I suggest that you read the books that I have mentioned to see the Jewish point of view. May I also suggest that you find a book called "The History of Messianic Speculation in Israel" by Abba Hillel Silver. He covers many of these questions in his book.

The basic problem is this, Steve. The Jews expected a Messiah who would come to change the world order – who would bring peace on earth and resurrection of the dead. Jesus of Nazareth came and died and did not do this. The prophets were each speaking in their own way about their hopes for the future.

Their prophecies were certainly not fulfilled in the life of Jesus – at least for the Jews. If anything, the world got worse rather than better. The Jews could not accept him as a Messiah, because he did not do what the Messiah was supposed to do.

7. We Jews believe that Jesus was a wonderful man who lived and died within the Jewish community. We believe that his followers made him into the only begotten son of God – but that his writings, as far as we can read them, were very similar to Jewish belief at the time.

Remember that the four Gospel writers had never met him – neither had St. Paul. They all came much later and wrote about him but had not been with him. Therefore, we do not feel that he was either a lunatic or a liar. We feel that he was a great teacher and rabbi who had great love in his heart.

I hope that that these answers are satisfactory and look forward to hearing from you.

Cordially,
Rabbi Cohen

Letter #3

My Response to the Rabbi

Dear Rabbi,

Thank you very much for responding to my letter and for saying such nice things about my 10-month-old daughter. I certainly want to raise Becky in a proper way and this means most of all a proper spiritual upbringing.

More than anything else, I want to teach her the Scriptural truths concerning God, man and man's relationship to God. That's why the subject I brought up in my last letter is so important to me. I believe that God wrote the Old Testament (through the prophets) to let us know what He expects of us.

And I believe with all my heart that a Messianic theme runs through every book of the Old Testament. I have to say that your answers to the questions in my last letter seem to be the modernistic Jewish answers which really don't reflect the traditional Jewish thought. I will attempt to back this up, using Jewish writings to do so.

1. You say the Hebrew word "almah" is recognized by 99% of biblical scholars as meaning young woman. I don't know where you got your information, but I could list here scores of Jewish and Gentile scholars who believe the word "almah" is properly translated "virgin."

And you can't deny, Rabbi, that the 70 top Jewish scholars who translated the Old Testament from Hebrew to Greek all thought that "almah" means virgin, since they used the Greek word "parthenos" – virgin.

Furthermore, I find that the word "almah" is used just seven times in the Old Testament and each time it refers to what can only be a virgin. So when you say "almah" is mistranslated, you are disagreeing with traditional Jewish thought.

One more thing before leaving this area. Looking ahead to chapter 9, verse 6 of the same book, one finds a description of this special child:

"For a child will be born to us, a son will be given to us; and the government will rest on his shoulders; and his name will be called Wonderful, Counselor, Mighty God, Eternal Father, Prince of Peace."

A child will be born who will be called "Mighty God"? Jewish commentators did not dispute the Messianic nature of this prophecy until modern times. As proof, let me cite the paraphrase of this passage given in Targum Jonathan:

"And there was called His name from of old, Wonderful, counselor, Mighty God, He who lives for ever, the messiah in whose days peace shall increase." (Targum of Isaiah)

Rabbi, I agree with you that you shouldn't read something into the biblical story that isn't there. However, I think it is just as dangerous to delete things that are there.

2. Now to your statement that the words "yachid" and "echad" mean the same thing. I have studied this intensively, and I have found that they definitely do not mean the same thing. "Yachid" is used in the Bible when an absolute, indivisible one is intended;

this is the word Moses Maimonides used to describe God in his second Principle of Faith. On the other hand, "echad" is used in the Bible for a compound, divisible unity, as, for example, when God says in Genesis 2:24, "And they (husband and wife) shall be one (echad) flesh."

In your letter, you say that "yachid" was simply the Medieval Hebrew meaning the same thing as the biblical Hebrew word "echad." This doesn't hold true, however, because Moses used both words in the Torah, so we see they were used concurrently. The only conclusion I can reach is that Maimonides was trying to cover up important biblical evidence for the tri-unity of God by calling Him an absolute one (yachid).

The biblical use of the word "echad," however, is by no means the only evidence that establishes the fact of the tri-unity of God. Beginning in Genesis, we find that a common name given to God is Elohim, a plural word. Why didn't Moses use the singular form, El? Also, many times we come across the use of plural pronouns for God as in Genesis 1:26: "Then God said, 'Let Us make man in Our image, according to Our likeness…'"

Even the sacred Jewish book – the Zohar – testifies to the truth of the trinity in its comment on the Shema: "Hear, O Israel, the Lord, our God, the Lord is one," (Deuteronomy 6:4).

"Why is there need of mentioning the name of God three times in this verse? The first Jehovah is the Father above. The second is the stem of Jesse, the Messiah Who is to come from the family of Jesse through David. And the third one is the way which is below (meaning the Holy Spirit who shows us the way) and these three are one."

3. I'm afraid my research doesn't bear out your answer that the "Suffering Servant" section is read in the synagogue.

According to the Jewish calendar of Haftorah readings, the 53rd chapter of Isaiah is not read. In point of fact, the Haftorah reading for Shofetim includes chapters 51 and 52 while the Haftorah reading for Noah, Sephardi ritual and Ki Tetze begins at the 54th chapter. Isaiah 53 is blatantly skipped over.

I think it is important to note that Rashi (11th century) was the first one to suggest that the Suffering Servant in Isaiah 53 represents Israel. Until then, the Suffering Servant was almost universally understood by the Jews as referring to the Messiah. By no means does Rashi's interpretation represent the traditional Jewish interpretation.

Here are a few references to back me up:

Rabbi Moshe Kohen Ibn Crispin (14th century) states that those who for controversial reasons apply the prophecy of the Suffering Servant to Israel find it impossible to understand the true meaning of this prophecy, "having forsaken the knowledge of our teachers, and inclined after the stubbornness of their own opinions."

Their misinterpretation, he declares, "distorts the passage from its natural meaning," for "it was given of God as a description of the Messiah, whereby, when any should claim to be the Messiah, to judge by the resemblance or non-resemblance to it whether he were the Messiah or no."

He also said, "I'm pleased to interpret the passage in accordance with the teaching of our rabbis, of the King Messiah ... and adhere to the literal sense. Thus, I shall be free from forced and far-fetched interpretations of which others are guilty."

Rabbi Elijah de Vidas (16th century) said: "Since the Messiah bears our iniquities, which produce the effect of his being bruised, it follows that whoso will not admit that the Messiah thus suffers for our iniquities must endure and suffer for them himself."

Rabbi Moshe el Sheikh, chief Rabbi of Safed, stated: "Our Rabbis with one voice accept and affirm the opinion that the prophet is speaking of the King Messiah, and we shall ourselves also adhere to the same view."

Isaac Abrabanel, a bitter opponent of Christianity, made the following statement about Isaiah 53: "Jonathan ben Uzziel interprets it in the Targum of the future Messiah; and this is also the opinion of our learned men in the majority of their Midrashim."

The original Messianic interpretation of Isaiah 53 survives to this day. It is preserved in Jewish liturgy for the Day of Atonement in the Musaf prayer:

"We are shrunk up in our misery even until now! Our rock hath not come to us; Messiah, our righteousness, hath turned from us; we are in terror, and there is none to justify us! Our iniquities and the yoke of our transgressions he will bear, for he was wounded for our transgressions; he will carry our sins upon his shoulder that we may find forgiveness for our iniquities, and by his stripes we are healed. O eternal One, the time is come to make a new creation, from the vault of heaven bring him up..."

Thus, it is obvious from the above prayer that the Jews of that era (8th century) believed that the Messiah had already come and were praying that He may come a second time.

Rabbi, I could go on and on, but suffice it to say that the Talmud, the Zohar, the Midrashim, and the Jewish Prayer Book all support the view that Isaiah 53 refers to the Messiah — not the people of Israel.

The modern Jewish answer can't be taken seriously by either the scholar or the casual reader. According to the Scripture passage in question, the Servant is described as "righteous," as "sinless," as a willing sufferer, and actually dying.

Not one of these statements can be applied to the Jewish people, as any unbiased person would be willing to admit.

4. Moving right along, we come to Psalm 22. You say the psalm doesn't mention crucifixion. Of course it doesn't! How could David use the word "crucifixion" when this manner of capital punishment was unknown to the Jews of his time?

But the psalm does say, "They pierced my hands and my feet" (Psalm 22:16). Sure sounds like crucifixion to me. In fact, the Midrashim (called the Pesiqta Rabbati) applies this psalm to the sufferings of the Messiah, so once again we find that traditional Jewish thought and modernistic Jewish thought are at odds with one another.

You're quite right in saying that David wasn't crucified; it was David's descendant, the Messiah, who was crucified. David predicts the manner of the Messiah's death in this psalm. Jesus even quoted the first verse of this psalm from the cross.

5. Now we move into the heart of our discussion – the need for a blood sacrifice to atone for our sins. You agree with me when you say, "The Bible does say that sacrifices are necessary." But then you say that the Talmud replaces sacrifices with prayer, good deeds and charity. While there are many fine and beautiful statements in the Talmud, I have to call a halt when the Talmud (a commentary written by men) starts contradicting the Bible. The Bible says:

"For the life of the flesh is in the blood, and I have given it to you on the altar to make atonement for our souls; for it is the blood by reason of the life that makes atonement" (Leviticus 17:11).

Who gives anyone the authority to say, "You don't have to obey that rule anymore. You can simply fast and do good deeds." Wherever you look in the Old Testament, you find His people offering blood sacrifices to become acceptable in God's sight.

The Hebrews had to apply the blood of a slain lamb to the doorposts of their homes if they wanted their firstborn to survive. As God put it, "When I see the blood, I will pass over you" (Exodus 12:13).

Much of the Torah – almost the entire book of Leviticus – is devoted to the subject of blood sacrifices.

Let's turn to the article on atonement given in The Jewish Encyclopedia:

"...the blood, which to the ancients was the life-power of the soul, forms the essential part of the sacrificial Atonement. This is the interpretation given by all Jewish commentators, ancient and modern, on the passage... The life of the victim was offered... as a typical ransom of 'life by life'; the blood sprinkled by the priest upon the altar serving as the means of a renewal of man's covenant of life with God... The cessation of sacrifice, in consequence of the destruction of the Temple, came, therefore, as a shock to the people... It was then that Johanan b. Zakkai declared works of benevolence to have atoning powers as great as those of sacrifice. This view, however, did not solve satisfactorily for all the problem of sin... Hence, a large number of Jews accepted the Christian faith in the Atonement by the blood shed for many for the remission of sins.'" (Rabbi Kaufmann Kohler)

The "Christian faith" mentioned above is actually the faith to which I adhere. May I suggest you read a book called Christianity Is Jewish by Edith Schaeffer (Tyndale House) for additional light on the subject. Hebrew Christians base their atonement with God on the biblical basis of "blood atonement sacrificially provided." Modern Jewish thought bases atonement on the Talmud, the word of man.

6. You say that Jesus did not do what the Messiah was supposed to do and for this reason the Jews do not accept Him as the Messiah. I disagree. The Bible says the Messiah would come first as a Suffering Servant, that He would die for the sins of His people, that He would be raised from the dead on the third day, and that He would return as a conquering King who would rule forever.

Multitudes of first-century Jews accepted Jesus as the Messiah; some estimates say that millions of Jews accepted Him. Others, however, desired and expected the Messiah to immediately set up His eternal Kingdom, directly in conflict with Scriptures that said the Messiah must first die.

Jesus did exactly what the Old Testament Scriptures predicted. What more could be asked of Him? Isaiah (chapter 53) and Daniel (chapter 9) both predict the death of Messiah and His resurrection. And Zechariah tells us something very interesting about the Messiah's return:

"And I (God) will pour out on the house of David and on the inhabitants of Jerusalem, the spirit of grace and of supplication, so that they will look on Me whom they have pierced; and they will mourn for Him, as one mourns for an only son, and they will weep bitterly over Him, like the bitter weeping over a firstborn" (Zechariah 12:10).

In other words, someday the Jewish people will be confronted by the Messiah "whom they have pierced" and will suddenly realize how wrong they have been to reject Him. This is the true Day of Atonement, when all of Israel will repent and turn to the Messiah.

Before you tell me I'm reading something into this passage that isn't there – that it isn't speaking of the Messiah – let me just quote from two respected and authoritative Jewish sources.

Commenting on this passage first is Rabbi Abraham ben Ezra (12th century):

"All the heathen shall look to me to see what I shall do to those who pierced Messiah, the son of Joseph."

Next is a rather lengthy quote from Rabbi Moshe el Sheikh, chief rabbi of Safed:

"I will do yet a third thing, and that is, that 'they shall look unto me,' for they shall lift up their eyes unto me in perfect repentance, when they see Him whom they pierced, that is Messiah, the Son of Joseph; for our Rabbis, of blessed memory, have said that He will take upon Himself all the guilt of Israel, and shall then be slain in the war to make an atonement in such manner that it shall be accounted as if Israel had pierced Him, for on account of their sin He has died; and, therefore, in order that it may be reckoned to them as a perfect atonement, they will repent and look to the blessed One, saying, that there is none beside Him to forgive those that mourn on account of Him who died for their sin: this is the meaning of 'They shall look upon me.'"

You tell me "it would be easy for me to pull verses from any book after I have a belief in a certain man as Messiah." I'd like to challenge you to do just that. A Mr. Fred J. Meldau has offered a $1,000 reward to anyone who can "produce any Christ, living or dead (other than Jesus of Nazareth) who can fulfill even half of the predictions concerning Messiah."

Looking at the Messianic prophecies in the Old Testament, we find that hundreds of prophecies were all fulfilled in the life of one individual – Jesus of Nazareth. Speaking of eight key prophecies, Peter Stoner, a mathematician, points out, "We find that the chance that any man might have lived down to the present time and fulfilled eight of the prophecies is one in 100,000,000,000,000,000" (Science Speaks, Moody Press). And the probability of any one man fulfilling all of these hundreds of prophecies is a number too large to write down.

To conclude this section, let me just add one more thing. You say that Jesus "came and died." But you make no mention of His resurrection. You may deny it really happened, but the resurrection is the best-attested event in history. Many books have been written on the subject, and it's much too deep to go into at this time. But let me quote former U.S. Supreme Court Justice Brewer:

"The existing evidence of Christ's resurrection is satisfactory to me. I have not examined it from the legal standpoint, but Greenleaf has done so, and he is the highest authority on evidence cited in our courts."

I am enclosing a copy of Simon Greenleaf's evidence for your edification (available free-of-charge from Book Fellowship International, P.O. Box 164, No. Syracuse, NY 13212). May I also suggest you read Who Moved the Stone? (Zondervan Press) by Frank Morrison. It's particularly interesting, because it was written by a man who started to write a book disproving the reality of the resurrection. By the time he was finished, he was a believer!

7. You seem to be unwilling to take a stand on whether Jesus was Lord, liar or lunatic, preferring to describe him as a "wonderful man." Does such a description fit a person who claimed to be equal with God, who forgave sins but said he had no sins of his own, who predicted his own death and resurrection?

No, I still maintain that your "wonderful man" option is implausible.

You tell me that "the four gospel writers had never met" Jesus and that "they all came much later." This is not true. Listen to the testimony of William F. Albright, who is considered to be the world's foremost biblical archaeologist:

"We can already say emphatically that there is no longer any solid basis for dating any book of the New Testament after about A.D. 80, two full generations before the date between 130-150 given by the more radical New Testament critics of today. In my opinion, every book of the New Testament was written by a baptized Jew between the forties and the eighties of the first century A.D."

Since the New Testament was completed so soon after the events it describes, the one element necessary to the creation of myths – time – was not available.

In effect, what you're saying is that the Gospel writers "made up" the Gospel accounts and that they bear little resemblance to what really happened and what Jesus really said. Considering the fact that most of the apostles and early Christians laid down their lives rather than their faith, your contention lacks credibility.

Could you imagine Mark Twain and all of his associates submitting to torture and death to prove that Huckleberry Finn really existed? Some of the top psychologists and experts in legal evidence have said that this just couldn't happen, and they have become believers on this very basis.

People might lay down their lives for a lie in which they sincerely believe, but they don't for a lie of their own invention.

You suggested that I read a couple of books by Samuel Sandmel. I have already read his We Jews and Jesus and believe he is quite honest when he admits, "I must be straightforward in saying that my approach is partisan; it is Jewish and not neutral."

All in all, I would say that Sandmel presents a very unbiblical account of which I disapprove. Please keep in mind that when I started investigating the claims of Hebrew-Christianity, I, too, was very biased on the Jewish side. I read Hugh Schonfield's book, The Passover Plot, and a number of other books by Jewish authors. After studying both sides, I came to the inescapable conclusion that the modernistic Jewish approach to the Scriptures is dishonest.

While I didn't want to believe the Christian side, the Old Testament evidence was all in their favor.

Now may I suggest you read a few books that will explain the Hebrew-Christian position better than I can. In addition to the books previously mentioned, read:

- *Judaism and Christianity, Are They the Same?* by David Bronstein (O'Neil, Oliver, MacKenzie, Inc.)
- *Jesus, the Jew's Jew* by Zola Levitt (Creation House).
- *Jesus Was a Jew* by Arnold Fruchtenbaum (Broadman Press).

- *The Bible, the Supernatural and the Jews* by McCandlish Phillips (Bethany Fellowship).
- *Hebrew Christianity: Its Theology, History and Philosophy* by Arnold Fruchtenbaum (Baker Books).
- *The Messianic Hope* by Arthur W. Kac, M.D. (Baker Books).
- *The Chosen People Question Box II* by Dr. Henry Heydt (Chosen People Ministries).
- *The Prophet Isaiah* by Victor Buksbazen (Spearhead Press).
- *Where in the World Are the Jews Today?* by James and Marti Hefley (Victor Books).
- *A Hebrew Christian Looks at Isaiah 53* by Sanford Mills (Chosen People Ministries).

If you haven't already guessed, I am a Hebrew Christian. I maintain that I can believe the Old Testament and in the Messiah it predicts, and still remain a Jew. While some Jews consider me to be a traitor, my question to them would be, "If Jesus really is the Messiah, who's the traitor?"

I'm not condemning you or anybody else, rabbi. God will judge us all in the end. But upon what basis will we be judged? According to the Bible, we will be judged by whether we believed God and believed in the blood sacrifice He Himself provided for the remission of our sins.

I've got something now that I never had before – the joyful assurance that I'm acceptable in God's sight through the shed blood of His Son. I base my views solidly on Scriptural ground. I read the Bible and I pray every day, something I never dreamed of doing in the past.

I consider myself a better Jew than before, because now I am a Jew in the biblical sense of the word. As you know, Abraham became "righteous in God's sight" when he believed God. He wasn't circumcised until later, and the Mosaic law came much later still, so neither of these things made him righteous. Now that I too believe God, I know that I am "righteous in God's sight" and that I am a complete Jew.

Rabbi, I wouldn't have taken the time to write this lengthy letter if I didn't care about you. Let me close by saying that many rabbis have put their trust in the Messiah and have gone on to do great things, never regretting their decision.

Have you seriously considered what the Bible says about the Messiah and about blood atonement? As Jesus said, "For if you believed Moses, you would believe Me, for he wrote of Me." My final question to you is, do you believe Moses?

From Deuteronomy 18:18-19:

"I will raise up a prophet from among their countrymen like you (Moses), and I will put My words in his mouth, and he shall speak to them all that I command him. And it shall come about that whoever will not listen to My words which he shall speak in My name, I Myself will require it of him."

Sincerely,
Steve Schwartz

Letter #4

The Rabbi's Final Response to Me

Dear Steve:

Thank you very much for your lengthy letter of December 29. I must say that I am happy that you have found happiness in your new faith. I don't think it is necessary for us to continue arguing.

You have taken certain sources and wish to read into them what you wish. I, as a rabbi, have spent over 16 years in deep, scholarly research of Judaism. If I would say to you that you are reading things into the Bible, you would not agree with me.

Since I respect your decision, I am most happy that it is meaningful to you. I, as a Jew, cannot accept that one who is a Christian still wishes to call himself a Jew. Why not be honest and say that you are a Christian, and leave it at that?

Furthermore, I think that Judaism respects Christianity's right to see God in its way. I, therefore, would not only ask but demand the same of those who are Christians. As I said before, I really don't think it necessary to continue the dialogue as I will not dissuade you from your belief, neither shall you dissuade me from mine.

I would only say that you are reading one type of literature and one type of book. To quote the sources such as Rashi and others and even begin to think that they would consider belief in Jesus as the Messiah is absolutely ridiculous. They never did and never would, and therefore should not be used in that way.

Faith should be a personal thing, and if you wish to believe that way, that is fine. Just please don't try to falsify what is truly Judaism to fulfill your personal needs.

I hope you continue to find fulfillment in your faith.

Sincerely,
Rabbi Cohen

Letter #5

My Final Response to the Rabbi

Dear Rabbi,

I'm disappointed you don't wish to correspond anymore, but I will respect your wishes. However, before we stop communicating, I just had to respond to some of the issues you brought up in your last letter. Don't feel obligated to write back. But if you do, your letter will be most welcome.

First of all, I considered this correspondence a legitimate form of expression called a discussion; I'm sorry you thought it was an argument. What I really object to is your implying that I'm not in your league because I haven't "spent over 16 years in deep scholarly research." The length of time spent in study doesn't necessarily mean anything. It certainly doesn't mean that you have the truth and that I do not. For one, I know of many people who have studied much longer than you and who have not reached the same conclusions as yourself. For another, I'm sure you'll admit that your studies consisted mainly of Talmudic rather than Old Testament studies.

The Old Testament claims for itself that it is the Word of God – more than 2,600 times, in fact. The Talmud never claims for itself such a distinction. It is merely a commentary on the Old Testament and a commentary on the commentary. Therefore, the Talmud is the word of man, and man has a good record of being wrong. Focusing one's study on the word of men, therefore, is a good way of perpetuating error. The men who wrote the Talmud lived thousands of years ago, long before the tremendous advances in biblical studies, Hebraic linguistics, archaeology and anthropology.

However, I must say it's remarkable how often the Talmud itself lends support to the Hebrew-Christian position. Alfred Edersheim's monumental work, *The Life and Times of Jesus the Messiah*, concludes with a lengthy appendix which cites hundreds of Old Testament passages considered by the writers of the Talmud to concern the Person or times of the Messiah, in agreement with the Hebrew-Christian position.

How can you suggest I'm no longer a Jew because I believe in the Old Testament and in the Messiah it predicts? You can call me anything you like, but that doesn't change the fact that I'm still a Jew. If you were to ask a Jew in Israel, he would say that we American Jews are not real Jews because we have not returned to the land of Israel. Orthodox and Reform Jews also look upon each other with disdain and engage in name calling. Remember that a Jew is one who is a descendant of Jacob through any of his twelve sons. Even your colleague, Samuel Sandmel, recognizes that Christianity is Jewish when he writes in his book, "If one rises above nomenclature, then, it is by no means incorrect to speak of Christianity as Judaism. Indeed, of the many varieties of Judaism which existed in the days of Jesus, two alone have abided into our time, rabbinic Judaism and Christianity" – *We Jews and Jesus*, page 151.

I, too, respect your right to see God in your way; I'm not forcing anything on you. All I'm trying to do is show you that one's faith must be based on truth. Neither sincerity nor intensity of faith can create truth. Faith is no more valid than the object in which it is placed. Believing doesn't make something true, per se, and refusing to believe a truth cannot make it false.

The real issue is the question of truth. Now, if Jesus is "God made flesh" – as the Bible says – He deserves the worship due God. If, on the other hand, Jesus is not God, worshiping Him would be a terrible mistake. So while I continue to respect your right to see God in your own way, surely you must see that we cannot both be correct. The basic issue, once again, is truth.

I disagree when you say that I cannot be dissuaded from my beliefs. If you could present pertinent facts refuting my position, I would have to listen. I agree with you, however, that I wouldn't be able to dissuade you from your beliefs.

I know of a Rabbi Max Wertheimer, of Dayton, Ohio, who came to believe that Jesus was the Messiah, and suffered some of the consequences. When his alma mater – Hebrew Union College in Cincinnati – found out about his belief in Jesus, his name was dropped from its list of graduates.

I maintain that your major objection to Jesus is not theological in nature but sociological.

In your letter, you accuse me of reading "one type of literature and one type of book." I would invite you, rabbi, to examine my personal library to see exactly what I've been reading. I have read – and continue to read – books which try to refute my beliefs.

I find in all such books one thing in common – a lack of respect for the Bible. I don't have to defend the Bible; it can stand on its own merits and has done so for thousands of years.

I believe that the Bible makes a true claim for itself – that it is God's written word. It is either God's Book about man and of infinite value, or it is man's book about God and of questionable value.

Oh, the book's ethics and moral standards are on a high plane. But you'll find much the same sort of thing in other religious and philosophical works. But if the Bible claims to be God's Word – but in reality is not – then it's a book of lies and deserves to be disregarded.

Furthermore, I never said that Rashi or my other sources believed Jesus to be the Messiah. Some may have believed but never said so for the sociological reason I gave above. More likely, they didn't believe because people who claimed to be Christians were, at their time, persecuting the Jews.

Let's take Rashi, for example. During Rashi's time, the Crusaders, with a cross in one hand and a sword in the other, were herding Jews into synagogues and burning them to the ground.

But were these Crusaders really Christians? They went against every teaching of Jesus. They claimed to love the king of the Jews, yet went around killing Jews. No, they weren't real Christians; they were counterfeits. But the Jews couldn't know that.

It is to be expected that Rashi's writings would reflect this animosity toward Christians. Consider the intellectual honesty of Rashi's statement on that crucial passage, Isaiah 53:

"Since Christians interpret Isaiah 53 as being a prophecy concerning Jesus, we maintain that this is a prophecy concerning the people of Israel."

As I have already pointed out in a previous letter, most of Rashi's contemporaries disagreed with his new interpretation. Furthermore, you cannot say with certainty that Rashi or my other sources "never did and never would" accept the Christian faith. By the things they wrote, I'd say that some of them did, but of course I cannot be certain.

I'm certainly not alone in my beliefs. Current estimates [1976] state that there are some 100,000 Messianic Jews (Hebrew Christians) at the present moment, but many more who haven't "gone public" with their beliefs.

You say that "faith should be a personal thing." That sounds reasonable on the surface, but your view is directly in opposition to the entire teaching of the Old Testament.

Somehow I can't remember God telling the Israelites: "Go ahead and build your golden calf; it makes no difference to Me." Or: "Go ahead and worship Baal; faith should be a personal thing."

Finally, you say, "I hope that you continue to find fulfillment in your faith." Thank you, rabbi, I will. Here's how I know this. My faith works because it is true. Many people think their faith is true because it works and gives them the feeling of closeness to God.

My feelings are probably indistinguishable from yours, but when it comes down to that final day, the day of standing before God, I want my faith to be grounded in God's truth. Subjective feelings of "fulfillment" are very weak grounds upon which to base your faith.

Why do people believe in absolutes in the field of mathematics and science, yet feel that "man's approach to God is up to the individual"? The Bible says there is just one way to God – through the Messiah, His Son, and no other.

My faith is based on the Bible and on historical, objective facts, not on feelings, nor the philosophical reasonings of men. After all, men are too prone to be wrong, so I cannot put my trust in them. I have to go along with King Solomon, the wisest man who ever lived, and say: "Trust in the LORD with all thine heart; and lean not unto thine own understanding" (Proverbs 3:5).

Sincerely,
Steve Schwartz

P.S. Rabbi, I really would appreciate hearing from you again. I hope you don't think I'm writing these letters just to be argumentative. You see, I'm proud of my Jewish heritage, but I'm not proud of the way we have strayed from God and from the Old Testament teachings.

My desire is to return to the faith of the Old Testament. The very essence, or core, of biblical Judaism is the Messiah. Without the Messiah, the only thing left in Judaism is tradition. And tradition cannot put us into a close relationship with God. Neither can tradition atone for our transgressions.

As for me, I can't reject the Messiah just because most Jews reject the Messiah. Since when is truth determined by a majority vote? The hundreds of Messianic prophecies in the Old Testament all point to one Person, and I can't reject Him without rejecting the prophets, the Bible and God for making a promise He didn't keep. I believe God did keep His promise and that the Messiah came right on schedule. I also believe I'm a better Jew, because I have accepted and believed God's Word. You see, I'd rather call Jesus "God" than call God "a deceiver."

Please feel free to write me again.

Postscript

The rabbi never responded to this letter.

As I mentioned at the beginning, I will let the letters speak for themselves and allow you to draw your own conclusions. May I just encourage you to read the Bible for yourself. Remember, both the Old and the New Testament were written by Jewish authors and were intended for a Jewish audience; they set forth the basis of the Jewish faith and are indispensable to the Jew seeking his religious heritage.

Determine the truth for yourself; it's too important a matter for you to depend on someone else's opinion, be it mine or a rabbi's.

Sincerely,
Steve Schwartz

The Old Testament Chapter Banned from the Synagogue

In *Dear Rabbi*, I made the claim that Isaiah 53 is never read in the synagogue, although the chapters immediately before and after it are read. The rabbi, on the other hand, claimed that Isaiah 53 *is* read. Who's right? The Haftorah readings in synagogues and temples all over the world are identical for the designated Sabbath days. The following chart reveals the way this "Suffering Servant" passage – beginning at Isaiah 52:13 and running through Isaiah 53:12 – is omitted from the Haftorah readings.

Ekeb	Isaiah 49:14 – 51:3
Shofetim	Isaiah 51:12 – 52:12
Noah	Isaiah 54:1 – 55:5
Sephardi Ritual	Isaiah 54:1-10
Ki Tetze	Isaiah 54:1-10
Re'eh	Isaiah 54:11 – 55:5

So we see that the Haftorah readings heard in the synagogue conclude at the very verse which begins the controversial "Suffering Servant" passage. and the readings pick up just after the 53rd chapter of Isaiah.

While some Jewish authorities state that the omission was not purposeful, others see a good deal of significance in the omission. For example, Herbert Loewe – a Reader in Rabbinics at Cambridge University and co-author with Claude Montefiore of *A Rabbinic Anthology* – had this to say on the subject:

"Quotations from the famous 53rd chapter of Isaiah are rare in the Rabbinic literature. Because of the christological interpretation given to the chapter by Christians, it is omitted from the series of prophetical lessons (HAFTAROT) for the Deuteronomy Sabbaths. The omission is deliberate and striking." (op. Cit. P. 544)

If you'd like to see for yourself if the "Suffering Servant" passage is skipped, you can find the schedule of synagogue readings listed in many Jewish calendars and in Jewish Bibles.

Make up your own mind as to why this chapter is omitted from the Haftorah readings. Also, ask yourself as you read this passage – written about 700 years before the time of Jesus: "Of whom does the prophet speak?"

Isaiah 53

1 Who hath believed our report? And to whom is the arm of the LORD revealed?

2 For he shall grow up before him like a tender plant, and like a root out of a dry ground; he hath no form nor comeliness, and when we shall see him, there is no beauty that we should desire him.

3 He is despised and rejected of men, a man of sorrows, and acquainted with grief, and we hid as it were our faces from him; he was despised, and we esteemed him not.

4 Surely he hath borne our griefs, and carried our sorrows; yet we did esteem him stricken, smitten of God, and afflicted.

5 But he was wounded for our transgressions, he was bruised for our iniquities; the chastisement for our peace was upon him, and with his stripes we are healed.

6 All we like sheep have gone astray; we have turned every one to his own way, and the LORD hath laid on him the iniquity of us all.

7 He was oppressed, and he was afflicted, yet he opened not his mouth; he is brought as a lamb to the slaughter, and as a sheep before her shearers is dumb, so he openeth not his mouth.

8 He was taken from prison and from judgment; and who shall declare his generation? For he was cut off out of the land of the living; for the transgression of my people was he stricken.

9 And he made his grave with the wicked, and with the rich in his death, because he had done no violence, neither was any deceit in his mouth.

10 Yet it pleased the LORD to bruise him; he hath put him to grief. When thou shalt make his soul an offering for sin, he shall see his seed, he shall prolong his days, and the pleasure of the LORD shall prosper in his hand.

11 He shall see of the travail of his soul, and shall be satisfied; by his knowledge shall my righteous servant justify many; for he shall bear their iniquities.

12 Therefore will I divide him a portion with the great, and he shall divide the spoil with the strong, because he hath poured out his soul unto death: and he was numbered with the transgressors; and he bore the sin of many, and made intercession for the transgressors.

NOTES

"Almah"

There are hundreds of Jewish and Gentile Bible scholars who believe that the prophet Isaiah was predicting the virgin birth of the Messiah. A list of the Jewish scholars alone would include such names as Dr. Sanford C. Mills, Milton Lindberg, Dr. Arthur W. Kac, Dr. Henry J. Heydt, Dr. Leopold Cohn, Dr. Jacob Gartenhaus and Dr. David L. Cooper. All of these eminent Jewish theologians believe that the Hebrew word "almah" is best translated by the word "virgin."

"Yachid"

The second Principle of Jewish Faith by Moses Maimonides: "I believe with perfect faith that the Creator, blessed be His name, is an absolute one (yachid) and there is no oneness in any manner like unto His, and that He alone is our God, who was, is and will be." Compare this with the words of the Shema, Deuteronomy 6:4 from the Jewish Scriptures: Hear, O Israel, the Lord, our God, the Lord is one ("echad" – a unity consisting of more than one part).

Isaiah 7:14

"Therefore the Lord himself shall give you a sign. Behold, a virgin shall conceive, and bear a son, and shall call his name Immanuel."

Lunatic, Liar or Lord

C.S. Lewis, the one-time agnostic who became a Cambridge University professor and brilliant man of letters, had this to say about the subject of Jesus being a "wonderful man":

"I am trying here to prevent anyone saying the really foolish thing that people often say about Him: 'I'm ready to accept Jesus as a great moral teacher, but I don't accept His claim to be God.' That is the one thing we must not say. A man who was merely a man and said the sort of things Jesus said would not be a great moral teacher. He would either be a lunatic – on a level with the man who says he is a poached egg – or else he would be the Devil of Hell. You must make your choice. Either this man was, and is, the Son of God: or else a madman or something worse" (*Mere Christianity*, Macmillan Publishing Co.).

The Rabbi Who Invented Rabbinic Judaism

On page 50 of this book, I referred to a first-century rabbi by the name of Johanan ben Zakkai – one of the most learned, influential and respected Jewish leaders of all time. In my quote from *The Jewish Encyclopedia,* I pointed out that he was the one who invented the way Jews have observed the Day of Atonement for the last 2,000 years: "The cessation of sacrifice, in consequence of the destruction of the Temple, came, therefore, as a shock to the people… It was then that Johanan b. Zakkai declared works of benevolence to have atoning powers as great as those of sacrifice."

Today, Jews observe Yom Kippur – the Day of Atonement – by fasting, by attending synagogue services and by doing works of benevolence … a practice started by Johanan ben Zakkai.

We have to ask how confident ben Zakkai was that his sins had, indeed, been forgiven by works of benevolence. Interestingly, his deathbed experience was described by Bernard Pick in *The Talmud: What It Is* (New York: John B. Alden, 1890). Here's the account given on pages 35-36 of that book:

"His disciples addressed him, 'Rabbi, light of Israel, thou strong rock, right-hand pillar, why dost thou weep?' He answered them: 'If they were about to lead me before a king of flesh and blood, who is today here and tomorrow in the grave, who if he were angry with me, his anger would not last forever; if he put me in bondage, his bondage would not be everlasting; and if he condemned me to death, that death would not be eternal; whom I could soothe with words and bribe with money; yet even in these circumstances, I should weep. But now I am about to appear before the awful majesty of the King of Kings, before the Holy and Blessed One, who is, and who liveth forever, whose just anger may be eternal, who may doom me to eternal punishment. Should he condemn me, it will be to death without further hope. Nor can I pacify him with words, nor bribe him with money. **There are two roads before me, one leading to Paradise, the other to Hell, and I know not by which of these I go** – should I not weep?" (Emphasis added)

If a man like this didn't know if his sins had been forgiven, how can any practicing Jew experience peace and the calm assurance that his sins have been forgiven? That's the tragic legacy of *rabbinic Judaism* – a religion based not on the Bible but on the Talmud and the teachings of men like Johanan ben Zakkai.

In contrast, *biblical Judaism* adheres to the teaching that sins are forgiven through a blood sacrifice – a requirement made clear in Leviticus 17:11: "For the life of the flesh is in the blood, and I have given it to you upon the altar to make atonement for your souls; for it is the blood that makes atonement for the soul."

Jewish and gentile followers of Jesus believe that their sins have been forgiven through a blood sacrifice. However, the blood that was sacrificed came not from a goat or a lamb but from Jesus, the Messiah.

As foretold by the prophet Isaiah 700 years before the sacrifice took place: "But he was wounded for our transgressions, he was bruised for our iniquities; the chastisement for our peace was upon him, and with his stripes we are healed. All we like sheep have gone astray; we have turned every one to his own way, and the LORD hath laid on him the iniquity of us all" (Isaiah 53:5-6).

About the Author

    I was raised in University City, a suburb of St. Louis, Missouri. Everyone called it "U City" for short, but it was also commonly known as "Jew City." Being raised a Jew in a predominantly Jewish area wasn't such a bad deal. Life was good, and it would get even better when I turned 13. After all, that's the age when every Jewish boy "becomes a man" at his bar mitzvah.

    After school each day, I attended Hebrew school. There I learned how to read Hebrew so I could read from the Torah at my bar mitzvah. I was not, however, taught how to translate anything. But that was okay with me; I wasn't planning on moving to Israel.

    With all this in mind, it wasn't surprising that I started to let my Judaism slide after my bar mitzvah. My Jewish education, so I thought, was complete. Soon, the Jewish traditions began to seem meaningless, and I found it difficult to have any interest in a nebulous God about whom the rabbis could tell me little.

    After my bar mitzvah, I maintained a few Jewish customs – including the day-long fast on Yom Kippur. While I really didn't feel that my sins were forgiven, I fasted because that's what Jews do.

    Although I never became an atheist or agnostic, I did become apathetic about my relationship with God – an apathy that would soon turn to animosity. When I was 16 years old, my father died at the age of 49. Two relationships were severed that day – the one with my father and the one with God. God was nowhere to be found in my consciousness, and I was content to leave it that way.

    And that's how it remained for the next 11 years ... until Chuck, a Christian coworker, had the audacity to tell me that Jews who don't believe in Jesus are going to hell. Suddenly the Jewish spirit that I thought had died long ago came to life! I fired back that Christians are idolaters who worship three gods. I also told him there was no way a Jew could believe in their Jesus-God! After all, the *Shema* clearly proclaimed, "Hear, O Israel, the Lord, our God, the Lord is one."

Chuck then asked me why God was mentioned three times in the *Shema*. He also told me that the Hebrew word for "one" in the passage (echad) actually means "unity" or a "oneness made up of more than one part." He told me that the *Shema* was one of the best proofs in the Old Testament for the Christian concept of the trinity.

He also asked me a number of other questions I was powerless to answer. All of these questions sparked within me a desire to "slug it out" in the intellectual arena. I was determined to show him that Judaism is the truth faith and that Christianity was false.

But first I had to prepare my case. And that required studying – a lot of studying. I started reading books about Christianity, only so I could find its weaknesses. I also read many books by Jewish authors to help me defend Judaism. I read books on archaeology, history, philosophy, theology – you name it. Since my commute by buses and trains took three hours every day, I had plenty of time to study.

I also started reading the New Testament and was surprised to discover that it was written by Jews and for a Jewish audience. I had started with the preconception that both the Old and the New Testament were filled with myths, allegories, scientific blunders and historical inaccuracies, but my preconceptions soon started crumbling under the weight of facts. Examining the Bible in the light of archaeological, scientific and historical source materials, I discovered that it was not only trustworthy, it had a supernatural origin. I was amazed to find that the ancient Jewish prophets had made hundreds of specific prophecies which were fulfilled to the letter hundreds of years later.

With this new respect for the Bible, I started examining the prophecies concerning the Messiah. My rabbi had told me we were waiting not for a Messiah but for a Messianic Age, a time of perfect peace. But the Bible describes the Messiah as a man. What was I to believe?

After I decided to believe the Bible, I was shocked to find out that there were more than 300 Old Testament prophecies concerning the Messiah, and all of them pointed straight to Jesus! I couldn't explain it away – the prophets foretold that the Messiah would be born of a virgin in Bethlehem, that he would be God's Son, and that he would be put to death by crucifixion before the destruction of the Temple.

Most shocking of all was the description of the Messiah presented in the 53rd chapter of Isaiah. This whole chapter – a detailed portrait of Jesus – had been written 700 years before Jesus was born. When I learned that this chapter is never read aloud in synagogues, I started to wonder: *Was this some kind of cover-up?*

After more than a full year of studying, my coworker then asked me the most crucial question of all. "How are your sins forgiven?" he asked.

I told him that we Jews fast and pray on the Day of Atonement. But Chuck showed me what the Jewish Bible says about obtaining forgiveness of our sins. There was no mention of fasting or doing good deeds. A blood sacrifice is needed (Leviticus 17:11).

"When God became a man and died on the cross," Chuck continued, "that was my blood sacrifice. What's yours?"

I knew that Isaiah 53:5-6 provided the answer: "But He was pierced through for our transgressions, He was crushed for our iniquities; the chastening for our well-being fell upon Him, and by His scourging we are healed. All of us like sheep have gone astray, each of us has turned to his own way; but the LORD has caused the iniquity of us all to fall on Him."

I didn't like where this was all leading me. Even after I reached the inescapable conclusion that Jesus was the eternal Son of God and the Messiah of Israel, my stubborn pride would not let me admit defeat.

However, it was while playing piano at a bar on July 3, 1975, that I suddenly felt God's presence. I somehow knew that if I entrusted my life to Jesus, God would forgive my sins and take care of my every need. Most of all, I needed a close relationship with God – not a new religion but the same kind of relationship that Abraham and David had experienced. That night, I thanked Jesus for being my atoning sacrifice.

From that day to this – nearly 35 years later – the far-off God I cared nothing about has been my closest companion. I now have the wonderful knowledge that my sins have been forgiven. I could never have found such peace had it not been for Jesus, the Jewish Messiah!

- Steve Schwartz, March 2009

Dear Rabbi

Printed in the United States
219994BV00001B/2/P